Glimpses of Earth

Also by Leo Lazarus and published by Ginninderra Press
Myanmar in Moments

Leo Lazarus

Glimpses of Earth

This work is dedicated to the people of the Kulin nation, upon whose lands many of these poems were felt and written. I pay my respect to their elders and ancestors as well as mine. I thank Country for giving us life.

Glimpses of Earth
ISBN 978 1 76109 274 9
Copyright © text Leo Lazarus 2022
Cover: Leo Lazarus

First published 2022 by
GINNINDERRA PRESS
PO Box 3461 Port Adelaide 5015
www.ginninderrapress.com.au

Contents

Trees With Faces	7
Sanctuary	8
Seeing Things	10
The Colour of Warmth	11
Reaching	12
Stings	13
Dark Arts	14
Immersion	16
Late Thanks	17
Drawn to the Moon	18
Earth's Lives	19
Does All Touch Tickle?	20
The Civil Roar	21
Honesty is Natural	22
Heaven's Glow	23
Rocks	24
Fallen Ibis	25
Treebones	26
The Frog's Beat	27
On the Wall of the World	28
A Beautiful Secret	29
Tell Me of the Waters	32
Desert Sound	33
Butterfly Cry	34
The Tree With No Sap	35
Shedding the Sea	36
Nightlights	37
Heavy Rain	38
My Life's Loom	40
Breathe the Seasons	41

Gaia's House	42
Messenger Birds	45
In Conversation With a Fox	46
Subtle Power	47
The Midnight Walkers	48
Rainbow Scent	49
DIY Grounding	50
Bird's-eye View	52
Gust	53
Bunnings	54
The Sunshower	56
Steep the Body	58
Lake Eppaloch	59
Starstruck	60
Twisting Old Gum	61
The Small World	62
The Termite and the Tree	64
Divide the Sun	65
Frangipani	66
Below the Mango Tree	67
The Shadow Splits	68
The Crossing	70
True Air	73
Waning Moon	74
Traps and Wings	76
Rescue My Guide	78
Far From the Clocks	80
Ancient, Timeless	81
Easily Influenced	84
Who Are You?	86
About the author	87

Trees With Faces

By the river stand the trees with faces
of gloom, shock and consternation
written of ancient lore on a stringybark script
expressions of decades not changed on a whim

By the river stand the trees with faces
of pursed lips and dark eyes
hairfuls of cockatoos and sap-bleeding ears
soothed as light fades with the cockie parade

By the river stand the trees with faces
listening to the muted clash of war in mid-river
as water against rock unceasingly rages
a timeless battle so familiar
as to be barely worth noticing
and when the owl's call pierces the night
under a bright hunting moon
it puts fear into all
except the trees with faces

Sanctuary

is a green moss glove
which shades you from harsh light
in cupped palms
enfolding you
cradling your precious form
massaging your sore limbs
to keep you well
in dappled glades and sheer-walled gullies
water driven through rock and dirt
she shelters you

Drop below the ridge's line
to lower eyes from humankind's
skyscraping city
adjust the gaze in subtle light
where natural constructions
minute magnified to magnificence
shroud the burgan
pock the muddy shore
cling to rocky secrets
webs and burrows
nests and failed quests
sanctuaries within sanctuaries

As the eternal beingness finds forms
step slowly down the ephemeral line
the secret place
with a beating heart
pumping for rain
pausing while the clouds regather
walking in the wrinkled palm
listening to the air flow
as she spins her hand
seeing the light come and go
and meeting the many beings
who too call this place home

Seeing Things

Two canoes pass with soft voices
rousing me from my reverie
flat on my back with straw hat over my face

They did not see me here
even as I sat up
a greeting half-formed yet not past my lips

They did not see me here
and they went down the river in canoes
seeing some things
and not others

Two ducks splash near the bank
and I sit, motionless
to see what can be unseen

But the first duck swings about, sounding alarm
the moment she rounds the bend
for I am not invisible

The Colour of Warmth

I walk with my back to the sunset
watching the forest receive it
with all the colours of warmth
terracotta tree trunks
and cherry-red rocks

Reaching

Somewhere there is a rock
trying to touch their toes
who won't realise they can
until their spine has broken
and somewhere there is a tree
stretching furiously to the sky
who doesn't see they are there
until they have fallen

Stings

I never realised how deep
dives a mosquito's sting
nor how deep their thirst
until their taught abdomen
swells and sweats blood
for I never watched them
with such interest
or wondered
does it hurt to sting
even a little?

Dark Arts

Until Earth spins
half one-twelfth or a shiver more
nature's clear lamp burns bright above
no crystal strewn cloud
or heaving damp mass
smothers the lucent glass dome

With such clarity I see the gradual turn
of the sun's dimming dial
so smooth that the disappearance
of colour from the world
is a slow surprise
a subtle trick for the eyes

The green-canopied gum
becomes a towering dark dream
bends its sacred form
over those nestled
on the hard plane
parting dirt from sky

What magic unfolds
that one rooted in rock
ironbarked and drought-hardened
fire scarred and storm whipped
is silken tipped soft
with a dancer's springy growth

While deep in the ground
roots pry and probe for the voids
impossibly small
between hunger and thirst
tentacles stretched through dense orange clay
in youthful persistence

The explosive reaction bold
in a cacophony of new-shooted leaf
how then this miracle
this transcendence of space
by something we call inanimate
without human traits?

Science's truth lies beneath the bark
a wooden straw imbibes nature's syrup
capillary actions stave off starvation
trees transport and transmute
fungal-concocted fuel
they don't have a heart

But what if it isn't water it's blood
and all of your science is just a dark art
if we could raise the last fallen tree
would it say
*I was alive
before you killed me*

Immersion

River, river, cool and near
what in your dark depths do I fear?
the swimming snake, the lurking eel
in my heart what should I feel?
but in diving in it's neither nor
only liquid joy and gum-ringed awe
the sun warm upon my back
my chest below a fly's attack
a rock's smooth coat of lime-green slime
a fleeting immersion from time to time
no, in sunny mid-river there is nothing to fear
deep in my heart I feel at home here

Late Thanks

The fire doesn't thank the spark
until the last ember glows in the dark

Sons don't thank their fathers
until they beyond them see no further

Clouds don't thank the ocean
until their raindrops are set in motion

Humans don't thank Earth
until they're enfolded again within that girth

Night doesn't thank day
until first light breaks its stay

Drawn to the Moon

Last night endless faces were drawn
into the shifting vortex of the moon
as the pattern of its sphere coloured
shifted to consume scraps of night sky
between the mass of cotton cloud

Today the trees talk loudly
about the people they saw
of the land and the beasts
tickling their roots
with a foot's soft drumbeat

Earth's Lives

Earth seethes and writhes with countless lives
humming and thrumming like immense bee hives
from the outermost reaches where the thin line
between planet and space is hard to define
through surface and crust to her innermost core
where molten rotation emits a deep roar
sending million-tonned tectonic plates
containing all our blindly named states
scurrying madly around the spinning globe
their grinding and crashing arresting rim-side earlobes

edges so often sources of wonder
age determined by forces which rip or sunder
from a freshly bared stretch of sea floor
to old mountain peaks beheld with awe
and on all of this regardless of age
fall raindrops and winds which slowly erase
wiping the land of the marks of old ink
until one distant day into the ocean they sink
for a youthful surface to rise from the morass
to again host life in every crack and crevasse

driven still by the core's thumping beat
in a rhythm of life which will always repeat

Does All Touch Tickle?

Do grass shoots tickle the horse's nose
as they nip and tug stem from root

Does hanging bark tickle the tree
before fierce winds tear it away

Do a fire's flames tickle the smoke
as it curls logs then falls to the sky

Do leaves tickle the mist
with their movement's swirling trace

Do snowflakes tickle the mountain
when they land on its melting rocks

Do clouds tickle the sky
as they fly above with a breath and a prayer

Does kelp tickle the ocean's cheek
while it dances for the tides

Do all things which touch
tickle each other

The way smoky clouds over distant mountains
tickle a life?

The Civil Roar

The howling wilderness meets the sound of civility
on the paddocked edge of a sprawling city
in a calling of crows and a song of the birds
a flow of sweet music and softly sung words
with the roaring cough of a Saturday mulcher
the thundering whirr of a police helicopter

when once a great clash
a thousand cockatoos and a single steel axe
now it's a brave flock of those
against a civil roar which needs no repose
we nature people know
which way it goes

Honesty is Natural

The lion tells the gazelle
I will chase
The gazelle tells the lion
I will run
The crocodile tells the wildebeest
I will hide
And the wildebeest tell the crocodile
We know

Heaven's Glow

Our knowledge of the heavens grows
As our roaring cities dim its glow

Rocks

I will show you the rocks are alive
They eat one molten meal then for aeons survive

Fallen Ibis

From the ibis on Falconer Street no soft drooping honk
in the morning mourning the nest that in the night
fell from the pine to the hard breaking road

The branch it sat upon no sturdier or stronger
than a bird's long broken wing
the fragile home is home no longer
and now the ibis cannot sing

Treebones

Tell me what you see
as when the blind regain their sight

a world rich in sound and
Earthly aromas of spring sent
to join the wind's caress of ear
is filled with the infinite intricacy

of a stand of silver-limbed trees
echoing the hillside's slope
with smudged green fingers reaching
for an electric sky which breathes lungfuls
of thick white cloud
all following the other

and the open bush's scar tissue
is a smooth and easy green
between mounds of treebones
patiently waiting for the march
of saplings young and fresh
to shade them dark
and let the moss become their flesh

again a no-man's-land
invisible

The Frog's Beat

I danced to the beat of the frogs
in the murky moon's cloud-veiled light
before the skies opened and its rays shone
the way into the bush's heart
where I said a prayer from in the dark
something to help me move
to the place where one is all
and all is one

On the Wall of the World

I am the fly on the wall of the world
who sees the beauty of the veined leaf
in its desiccated colourless moment
before fire consumes it

I am the eel in the crevice
watching the blazing last glory of the reef
there with fish and coral-coloured fin
as the ocean's fringe thins and fades

I am the eyes in the undergrowth
watching men with heavy treads
trample budding wildflowers by the way

I am the hawk in the sky
soaring clear over the subtle vast plain
surveying the toll of a year without rain

A Beautiful Secret

In the forest she felt vibrant
alive with a panacea of tropical colour
vivid lush glistening green
her body a glow of collected shades
unique to the day
and the light of the glade

An orchid-blue shoulder
velvet-red leg
brilliant fungus-orange tail
and an eye full of early morning blue sky
set her apart from the creeping
monotoned undergrowth creatures

Placed her in the realm of the butterflies
the place where time floats
for in the world of beauty
everything changes fast
while for the world in the dark below
time oozes thick and furtive creeps

When night comes and hides the sun
her brightness and her colour fades
flanks ashen grey and legs coal black
eyes two moons in a blackwater lagoon
until lucent lids enfold the lens
as bands of cloud sweep over sky

She dreams without colour
and so passes the night
awaits a fresh day's radiance
to break through canopy cover
bring tinges of green back to the glade
see the fungus emerge from fallen branch bends

Petals unfold with their dreams untold
colour floods back into her flanks
her feet her legs and lastly her eyes
in that light filled moment
she felt electric
willing to die enough to be alive

Her colour kept flowing
rising with the sun
while she moved carefully knowing
her life and her body's ephemeral wax and wane
her beauty and myriad colourful ways
were hers alone

No one could see
through her perfect disguise
part her from the foliage
untangle her limbs
her vivid vibrancy could never be freed
from the old forest

Yet each day she chose
to paint with leaf-filtered light
from a dappled tree's palette
that was her life
a chameleon's
beautiful secret

Tell Me of the Waters

Tell me the waters are soft and bland
when they rip and sunder rock and land
in driven air they scream and tear
root from ground and leaves like hair

on barren shores they chew and crunch
eat sand afore the cliffs they munch
slide and wrap their icy tongue
round pebbles loose then soon undone

sent tumbling to the liquid maw
destined rocks for the unlit shore
into the dark of an endless gullet
filled with ships and blinded mullet

shattered timbers and whitened bone
settled in a timeless home
tell me the waters are soft and bland
when they up and lick a fisherman's hand

tickle his leg and spray his head
then pluck him whole from on the ledge
then call them calm and soft and bland
when firm upon high ground you stand

the body of water has no sign
of its power or its great design
until a movement deep fills every space
then sharp the fright on a fisherman's face

Desert Sound

What is the sound of desert ground
your heart's pumping stop and start
a human drum begun
before you ever sighted light

What is the sound of desert air
a thinly whispered promise
susurrating spinifex
thorny and fine

The sound of midnight ice
and midday fire
a bell ringing over a horizon
which can't be found

Butterfly Cry

The magpie leaps from ground to air
beak claps shut on soft winged butterfly
they hop a bird length away
let out a melodic cry
and I can't tell
if it's of the magpie
or the butterfly

The Tree With No Sap

The tree with no sap
stands alone grey leaved in the grove
branches thin and brittle
bark weathered and peeling
yet alive

breathing in shallow fits and starts
when the heavy clouds break for the sun
limp canopy swaying in wind
whispering and groaning
never roaring like those of its kin

its buds have long stopped flowering
its birds have long flown the nest
the bark-sheltered grubs have scurried away
yet the tree with no sap lives
old, weary, grey and thin

bearing the elements
until its fortune fades

Shedding the Sea

The water is rushing off the rocks
great sheets of stone shed the sea
lifted bodily from the depths
hungry for the kiss of air and sun

Ceaseless breakers pound the gates
of the outer reef's coral rim
that far living wall which keeps the peace
between harbour and ocean

Sharp-beaked herons watch the rapids
like a pair of salmon-hungry bears
and on the outcrop one wrestles a fish
skinny and tenacious as it wraps itself
around the very thing that caught it
to hold a little longer to what it knows of life

People swim to the island and yell and scream
coconut oil wafts from my skin
palm fronds hang low in the breeze
shells crawl along the rock pools
on hidden hermit limbs

The water is rushing off the rocks
even as they sink onto their beds
the herons are statues
until the moment they follow their beaks
and are lightning

Nightlights

To say the burning lamps of the night sky
flicker only from the past
is to give substance to the illusion of time
for they join the witness
as priceless jewels
in the starlit here and now

Heavy Rain

The rain pelts
pouring pellets
hard dense ovals
fallen out of shape
spattering
exploding Earth

joining water
with a smacking din
driving streams
brown pools with purpose
sheets of liquid
going all to river

soaked children slide
over the flowing yard
tin roof drum
an endless thunder
vision blurred
to the distance of an aquarium

faster now the river
faster she flows
then the drum stops
the far bank exists still
the boy's boat
a sandal on a string

sinks
and the trees
are new green
misty distant
shedding water
after heavy rain

My Life's Loom

The full moon, my life's loom
threads spun around the spectral sphere
of this hovering ephemeral
ethereal being
illumined and lost
by half menstrual turn
as I cast around in the dark
and sing on my haunches in the light
a frog like any other frog
crouched by a tall tree
the moon my loom
my anchor half won
my drifting undone
my moon

Breathe the Seasons

Earth inhales
deep livening singing breath
in spring
holds it in tight drawn lungs
red in the face
time long and slow in summer
exhales with cool relief in autumn
and holds those rock-encased bellows
empty and frozen and motionless
in winter

Gaia's House

Gaia lives in a cave warmed by a ribbon of magma
threaded through the floor
its orange glow gives her hair an inner life
and her eyes a bright fire
a pool brims with water trickled down a glistening rock wall
into the glow worm reflecting depths

When she sings the walls hum
the vaulted ceiling of her home
perfectly formed for widening sounds
and when she bathes in the clear water
she dries by the magma stream
steam lifting from her body into the darkness

She sometimes feels the air stir
as the winds above push and pull the liquid invisible
of the tunnel which loops through the rock
and emerges to her garden
which she tends and neglects with equal love
in the hope its creatures will toil while she is away

Sometimes long periods pass without an urge to see the sky
and when she emerges to see destruction
where she began with creation
she breathes a fierce breath
belly hot air sweeps the land
scorching all beings alike

And perhaps the next time she returns
dousing them in flooding rain
in the hope of waking the senseless guardians she appointed
in a time when they worshipped her full well
when she was honoured by their humility
and their valour fore their shame

They were not perfect these now old ones
they battled and quarrelled and drew each other's blood
but in their senselessness still they honoured her
they paused before a kill and stopped a moment after
promised to understand her kind
to know her sisters and her brothers

Some met the family of the divine
while others fell away
as generation grew generation they forgot
who blew the wind and who wept the rain
and one by one they lapsed
into the darkness of insanity

While the memory of Gaia ran like a fish to spawn
against the unconscious river
leaping from one bloodline to the next
the few keepers born into a different time
set apart from their brethren
by their heavy knowledge of truth and ignorance

The guardians lonely pining for their mother
fleeting unions sorely short
waiting for the time
in their valour and their grief
when Gaia's blessing renewed
the joy of the ancient line

Messenger Birds

The call of two yellow-tailed black cockatoos
rang from the sky
and the old man stopped his work
to lean on his shovel
among the clay and the rock
and look across the valley
where the birds flew wingtip to wingtip
seeing the face of the woman he loved
who wasn't for him

In Conversation With a Fox

You're not supposed to be here
I said
Neither are you
Said the fox
and we slinked away from each other
tails between our legs
the bush ours
but not ours
home
but not home
the animals afraid of our tread
nostrils flaring at the wind
carrying our foreign bodies
tail thump warning and
bird throated cry
as the strangers pick their way
through the dense bush

Subtle Power

Do you see the subtlety
of the lightning bolt
as it threads its way through the air
making the million connections it must make
jumping from one void to the next
as carefully as a tree root picking a path
which will find Earth's nectar
in its own time
it all happens so fast
for our feeble blinded eyes
do you see the subtlety
of pure power?

The Midnight Walkers

This is for the loners
the sole midnight bushwalkers
who strip synthetic clothing
to walk naked in the moonshine
who feel the spider's web catch their chest
hold them for a moment
then break and join their passage

Rainbow Scent

Can you smell the rainbow?
like rain and sudden sun
metallic sky and yellow light
day and night in one
a flashing arc of colour
gentle brilliant wonder

DIY Grounding

How to ground yourself
another question left unanswered in this culture
so I get some sun, fall asleep outside, wake groggy
cook, eat, water the garden
piss at the base of the orange tree
pick up my axe and make a clean finish
of a messy job

The parasitic pittosporum I cut down months ago
here through no fault or endeavour of its own
was still living, leaves green and drinking
through a shattered straw
where the trunk had split and the branch
keeled and collided with the slope

I sliced it away from its source
to hasten the inevitable death I began
the axe sat well in my hands
motion smooth and crisp
so I swung through a dead stringybark limb
chips flying with the ring of steel and hardwood
across the valley

Then I came into my body, slowed
lay in the knee-high spring grass
heads full of sweet seed
and looked at the treetops catching the sun
the little flying ones spiralling around a dead trunk
insects unknown among the famous and infamous
dragonfly blue and droning mosquito

Western commotion of ravens full chase
follows a silent wedged-tail's low flight to the east
I lie on Earth's shoulder
take in her air
empty my eyes
and dissolve into the ground

Bird's-eye View

When birds look through our windows
to see feather on feather within
a peacock's worth in a vase
an eagle's in a jar
cockatoos and rosellas bursting from a pot
do they see olden greed
the paradise bird hunters of now and then
do they see morbid grim
as if we glanced a window to row of human limbs within
or do the birds see treasured gifts
wind given and air spun
their light message of beauty innate
the trappings of wonder
for their Earthbound kin

Gust

Wind in trees
canopies shifting in the dark
gust travels swift and invisible
rattling branches and tearing leaves

The rattle is not alone the gust's
but the clamour of hard limbs
beating each other in their fury
or their ecstasy

Gust outruns their shimmering action
sweeping dust and browned detritus
stale flower blossom and bark fine fibre
before them

Driving and dropping from one place to the next
pouncing from canopy to canopy
floundering in the thickest
heedless of the bat-worn and bare

Until many miles and many hills
crested and sailed and crested
sap the rushing air their breath
and gust ceases

All the trees stand still
dust and pollens settle
branch backs away from branch
twig from twig
and Earth begins to speak
in the silence

Bunnings

Bunning's carpark grey sky
grey hard concrete
green shed
forest green
green of moss and leaf and
old grass splitting slab and sky

Cold wind
cutting my clothing
perched on a mulch bag
head stuffy and low
crisp leaves scuttling over the ground
voices shooting the breeze

Rain spitting early warnings
sunny day now to inside
from outside the vast shed
where products are ripped
from Earth
only to be loaded back
on her open wounds

A hilltop removed for clay
carefully worked into pond underlay
beside the hardwood deck
cut from the valley by a whirring blade
instant turf in thick rolls
skimmed off grass frog ground
salt scraped from a desert lake
bagged and poured into ceramic pools
chrysanthemum fields yellow white
beheaded, ground, now bottled pesticide

This is the shed
where Earth's gifts are taken
remoulded, repackaged and forsaken
traded for dollars and TV show dreams
in a forest green place
we call Bunnings

The Sunshower

The sunshower came through blue skies
blown in on shining droplets
small suns throwing speckled light
over the clear vault

Daystars gliding in
not hammering Earth
but drifting into her grasp
a cloud's brilliant homecoming

Life glistens when rain and sun fall together
small white moths dance between the drops
as I stand and sing with wet sunballs
kissing my naked skin in the sunshower

A rosella and a lark perch a branch apart
watching the land steam with joy
as it drinks life in
and the burgan's flowers are whiter for the wash

The slick puddled liquid
draws popping hissing bubbles
from the soaked timber table
squeezing old air from wooden pores

Little spider floats past then hitches
the beginnings of a web to my arm
hardy beings don't despair when anchors shift
but search anew for their foundations

Magpies glide in
sing an arriving song
then feast on what the wet meadow brings
myriad bounties of the sunshower

Steep the Body

Slowing is in the steeping
of the body in the great world
it's keeping an eye on the ants
ground dwelling attendants
swarming the magpie's outstretched wings
so their flight is smooth

It's looking at life more carefully
giving attention to your past ignored
shedding layers in evening sun
riding the pause between tree's conversations
grass stems waving in the wind

It's the tickle of ant legs
on rarely bare skin
flittering comets white butterfly winged
the spinning shadow of a travelling leaf
over a purple-flowered field
prowled by sure-footed birds

Heads dipping and darting
stalking and gulping and scouring the dirt
the grass in its growing shining path
of allegiances and networks underground

Life in a clearing
busy yet slow
met face to face
eye to eye
and body to body

Lake Eppaloch

A stop off the road
on the shore of Lake Eppaloch
pricked by low reed shoots
and the six-footed ants
who carry parts of it away
to treasure in their caves
where the gold of a dragon's lair
is a ripe head of grass seed
even King Midas could eat

The wind runs up the lake
carrying a gull to the west
and promises of rain no farmers trust
redgums shade the roaring way
between the naked hills
and where the water too long wet their roots
grey chaotic sentinels stand
waterlined trunks and unbarked arms
anchors for the winged and the finned

Starstruck

The magic of stars
Is that they still surprise you
Even when you know they've always been there

Twisting Old Gum

Twisting old gum
bark wrapped like a
bedsheet on a restless
summer night
when the air is thick
heavy before it fills
with soft rain

The trunk a shifting body
turning from east to west
then gazing back again
sunset left in white rings
great stripes diagonal
on the coat
remembrances of the fevers
which come then slowly go

Old tree twisting
spiralling out of Earth
dancing to the heavens
a tortured kind of verse
of sun-worship and
unquenched thirst
all told in a bark painting
canopied by wind-stirred leaves
and growing longer every day

The Small World

I woke to a pink brush
sunrise swept over the trees
slept until the sun
lashed my bare neck
awake and wanting me to know
his stinging benevolence

I resisted his call
crawled into the shade
foetal by the mattress base
cracked an eyelid
and entered the small world
the big world lands on top of

Ant road by my side
rapid beings decisive
stone still pause then dart
body-length over body-length hindered
grass stem a steel pole
stone fragment a blinding hillock

A giant bursts from the plain
iron toned armour over a bulbous back
legs pumping this barrel onto the way
the ant action of one mind
has the vanguard of a small army
clambering over the great intruder

Pumping legs rocked
rumbling form unbalanced
careening to their side before righting
trundling desperate on
fleeing the highway of devoured, slow beings

Over the plain with a darting farewell
of the final ant
who jabs at their flank
until a boundary is met
for ant, territory
for giant, end of terror

Traffic flow returns
the sun thins the leaf shadows
and the ground is awake

The Termite and the Tree

If you doubt the accumulation
of the potency of small efforts
consider the termite and the tree
the one smaller than the fingernails
tipping your arms which barely wrap
the smooth-skinned eucalypt's trunk
who does not stop to ask
if its tiny tearing jaws will strip
the wooden flesh faster than the rings
of changing seasons will hem them in
encasing them in a groaning coffin
with red gum hardened at their door
who tunnels and bites and chews
a maze through their timber wilderness
listening to the tree's voice as it speaks
in the cold of night and the heat of day
exchanging words with the air rushing
in and out of its lungs
and dancing with the wind
until one day the tree's voice breaks
its heart cries out as daylight floods in
and the termite sees the scale of its uncreation
years of labour to reverse and remove
undoing the tree's work from within
inhabiting the fortress limb by limb
until tree's trunk grew too thin
to continue the talk and the dance with the wind
and they fell
for a cumulation of many small things

Divide the Sun

Sea magic to split the sun
show its glory a thousand times
from creased mirror to hidden lives
suns drifting with the wind
with the currents
with a hymn
dancing on the glass flats
where wet sand runs with water
the sun jumps from the breaking wave
to meet the mirror's mirror there
wash its shadowless form away
return a thousand times to the plains
which glitter shine and shimmer
beyond the gulls and boats
beyond island bulk and rock
to fall off the sharp horizon
and meet the cool relief
of unbroken sky

Frangipani

Frangipani blossoms from my navel
my birth route cut and tied
now breathing the thick sweetness
of yellow and white five-petalled life
which swings me away on the flight of memory
only deep scent brings

The question of what brought me
to a specific part of time
is no stepping stone crossed river
but a cloud which coalesces in the sky
vapours invisible making filmy beds
to float in full rest

To tropical places
to islands and shady trees and paths
lined with the blossoms
of the yellow-white wonders
adorning ear and breast and navel
frangipani

Below the Mango Tree

In the shade of the mango tree
the buffalo who know the little girl lay
on hard packed earth worn smooth
by their stone-sleek hides

Their tethered reach leant weight
by the chicken's ruffled path
of well turned soil pecked clean
along an arc around their home

Calf long-haired and short-horned
its young growth of moss not worn
the rope harried with knocking swords
against its driven post

A hoof lazily thrust at the chicken's freedom
so it takes its space and flutters on
while the mango spreads out far and low
stooping to soothe the hot sun's glow

Tasselled switches flay the breeze
but flies are few for these are river stones
daily washed by their master
in the bamboo-lined stream

Walked for their bath
milked for our tea
resting nose to nose
below the mango tree

The Shadow Splits

Evening sun to narrow eyes
heat shells
shadow hairs
kiss necks
create two of everything
polarise the east from the west
make one half too visible
another disappear
in a way which questions the third dimension
for if half the world's face
can close like a weary eye
how can the certainty of the far side
the full circle joining of a tree's trunk
be any more than guessed at?

This I ponder
this the fairy wrens ignore
sure footed in their trunk circling spiral
deft in the fan-tailed entrance
then exit from the black eastern reach
this the hills belie
improbably solid
impenetrable for all their sun-soaked deceptions
and the cherry ballart smirks
for its trunk is rippled black
from east dawn to west dusk
while my compass needle spins
they take their cue from firm ground
steady themselves
working toes into clay
and carefully unfurl
bodies moving up and away

The Crossing

Run to the river
shirtless to the still hot seven o'clock sun
fast and light down the block
small sharp steps on the slope
an eye for sticks which move
shimmy over the plank by the dam
vault the vacant wombat hole
spring slow and steady up the hill
bounce from toe to toe
elastic calves propelling the body

Breathe deeply now
where it's harder to move along the flat relief
atop the climb
than it was to move up it
drop fast again
crickets and stones leaping into the grass
false serpentine intimations
left behind in a tumbling of legs
rolling over faster and faster
to hit the flat

Glance the roos distant
the reeded dam close
climb with the knowing of water ahead
making this doing the easiest part
legs strong pump and shine
crest and fall a rocky scree
a curving path below the timber tall
duck the cypress marking a road's end
lope the pine-needled land
to laughing waters close

Long and free now leg swings by leg
body falling into liquid dreams
when the dust black being appears
a silken muscle weaves over hard-packed ground
with force enough to shudder tired legs
in a three-step halt
split second pause
and rewind the falling motion
draw a dozen silent paces
into the past

As if their sinuous motion in one direction
reverses and returns time
which disappears in the colourless voids
between the olive-green and pale yellow stripes
of the tiger morphed into sleek sinew
flowing from path to bush
the last wave of a sudden flood
to vanish in grass stem shadows
the pendulum swings
frozen legs melt into movement

To dive and slice the surface
glide in muddied darkness
breath held and heart straining
pounding at its ribbed cage
the feared thing looked for since home
coming the moment the eyes closed
the moment the mind launched itself
from body to river embrace
to join them in communion
with the tiger snake

True Air

It is night
the distant call of frogs
comes through the stillness
four beats
a long pause
a forgetting
four beats

Animal feet crunch leaves over the flat
summer's thick mat of dry eucalypt sheddings
round red box colours from fresh-snipped green
brittle bleached browns
cirrus cloud sunset pinks

Voices drift through the screen door from the backyard
footsteps from the kitchen
clicking insects from the shadowy trunks
cars from a far off road
gentle rushing
the pair of dogs over the valley
bark with the valley over

All of it immediate
in air which speaks the truth
not changing the shape of their waves
as if it is nothing
invisible
air

Waning Moon

It's a long time fore the moon
the fading of her fullness
less to do with her size or brightness
than with our eyes closed to seeing her
sleeping while she shines in the wee hours
waning yet not gone

Though a week might pass
where we've missed something
but known not what
until a clear morning's sight of a crescent
pale and slight against a teacup-blue sky
wakens us from our young day's dream

The soft something we've missed
which stayed up later than early for us
if only we raised our eyes to her
in the times when she's not the fire of night
those when she doesn't boldly wrench the gaze
for wonder at the swirls and mysterious darknesses
under her pearl and glass eyes

If only we didn't think her beauty gone
the moment her fullness goes
not see her as a beauty past her prime
month upon pattern-breaking month
cherished her descent to her rest
sang to her through the dark nights

Knew of her hidden places
even when we could not join her there
raised our eyes to blue skies
in morning search for her lingering touch
cool and soothing in a sun-washed vault
empty of starfire and secrets

Waited her growing powers
with patience born by love of the whole
as she wanes then slowly waxes

Traps and Wings

There is a life or death struggle
raging two feet away;

One being sets a trap
finds a quiet corner and watches
one being goes about their living
drawn this way and that

Following one sense or another
vibrant and active with the young night
and the little corner of it awash in lamplight
a nightspot for the awake and the free

Until its smooth sequence of wingflaps
each up and down an act of defiance
the acts of a course through limitless air
is jagged to a graceless halt

One wing on the down or the up floated too near
the invisible trap and the watcher in the corner

It's not so much panic
that makes the watched beat so hard their wings
body writhing round the coil
as a certainty that limitlessness is their right

That every sense they have goes to movement
that the night is young
and they are not yet old

So the wing hooked on this fine line
on a downbeat or maybe the up
keeps beating but it's their shell which flaps instead

The watcher knows the delicacy of their web
can feel it twang and stretch through their legs
blinks a black needlehead eye
clambers to the frayed entwining
where mercy looks to be one thing but is another
for embraces aren't freeing while they last

The watcher's slow dance
has left the flyer flightless
wings hard bound each to the still other
only feeble legs can kick and rend the shroud

The watched becomes the watcher
captivated by the captor
who spins and twists and pulls
their find to a sheltered place
a cornice and bedhead-bound cave

Thickens the shroud until even legs grow still
to truss their packaged prey
and there they wait
growing old as night becomes day

Rescue My Guide

Another freed from the trap unnatural
blue-tongue in a wire mesh
body cool but flexing under my sad hand
until I felt for life
a hopeless thought for those unblinking eyes

My finger brushed their chest
a foreleg gently moved
and there was life
surprising life, fragile life

I the carer chosen for I passed through
called by their desperate spirit
treading a place few people tread
off the path and in the scrub

On the phone for help
a log pillow placed under their dangling head
race to collect the wire cutters
return full of purpose

Snip the wire away
withdraw the creased belly
catching legs and barely mobile form
to rest under my shirt

Build a log house
a shelter for the night
nestle them in
sing a song for their health

May you be well ancient being
reptile friend
may I be your rescue
and you my guide

To go carefully on my way
for not all we wish to fit in the world, fits us
not every temptation is worth pursuing
and help will come
to those who call

Far From the Clocks

How time distorts
when far from the clocks
is always a joyful wonder
three days ago
is such a long time
right now
I entered the timeless once more
listening to the fire talk
in their crackling hissing voice
which shoots parts of themself into the night
when they shift and laugh
parts of themself
collapsing and coalescing
into a yet more intense heart
as we speak our truths
our shadows and our lights
into their magmic eye
and burn brighter still

Ancient, Timeless

In a culture of forgetting
we retell the same story
with different names
and don't know quite why
everything new looks so familiar

We call this place
ancient and timeless
at the same time
and don't know we can write
our future
and our past
together

Now,
I was born of fire and water
for the sun exploded the day
I slipped easily into this world
and I never understood
why the moon is woman
until I saw my lover's skin
luminous under her light
so both glowed the same

I never understood
why the sun is man
until my body was seared by his kiss
and I turned my sight from his eye
to lose my way

For it takes more than only sun and moon
to raise the young to age
a field of stars revolving
storytellers for the still dusk
enlivening the lonely firmament
until the slow brightened dawn

In my future
I was told what my gifts were
taught to seek
shown to share
loved to love
by a sun and moon born family
who knew the way home

In my future
they wounded me with fire
and cut me with ice
for I had never suffered
more than the scrapes of boyhood
so I became a man

In my future
the stars told me
how the sun loves the moon
the moon loves the sun
and Earth was born

In my future
they said, *listen*
and I opened my ear
while they sang
their ancient timeless creation
until they said
sing!
and my future
became my past

Easily Influenced

The dandelion head
lofted from her stalk
on the first whim of a still morning
heady with her whirling flight
tumbled the way a sphere rolls
forever appearing upright
whether or not north is south
or east is west

She flashes in dazzling bursts
on for sun
off for shadow
gliding along a well treed ridge
dipping for the coldness
of marbled naked stone
rising into the hills' warm pockets
where giants rest their winter hands

When the ground runs
into heaving seas
she dances in the surf
tickling white-capped fiends
with her silver hair
catching the spray in her arms
and darting away from the gaping mouths
which collapse where she and the wind had been

Tossed and turned and flung
with a spinning globe's composure
which can't cry for imbalance
taken by the wind and sun
surrendering to the dance
ignorant of her place of rest
so on landing beyond the dunes
by a patch of soil calling her name
she shed her perfect circles
and came home

Who Are You?

Who are you
when the sun dies

Who are you
when the moon goes dim

Who are you
when the light fades

Who are you
when Earth falls
into the void?

About the author

Leo Lazarus is a writer and poet who rediscovered his wonder with a tree-change. He captures the essence of bush landscapes, movements and life. In the process, he finds parts of himself hiding in the treetops and beneath the moss. He is passionate about encouraging others to explore writing as a tool for personal understanding and for opening our senses to the magic of life.

www.ingramcontent.com/pod-product-compliance
Lightning Source LLC
Chambersburg PA
CBHW062142100526
44589CB00014B/1669